Contents

On the Case

When the police need to find someone who has gone missing, they know who to call. A four-legged detective arrives at the scene and is ready to work! This police dog has an amazing tool for finding missing people—its nose! The dog sniffs the missing person's shirt. Then, it runs off to follow the scent. Before long, the heroic dog has found the missing person.

Police dogs are also called K-9s. This is because it sounds like the word *canine*, which means dog.

Heroic Dogs

POLICE DOGS

by Megan Cooley Peterson

Consultant: Denise Sanders,
Director of Communication, Search Dog Foundation

BEARPORT PUBLISHING

Minneapolis, Minnesota

Photo credits: Cover and 1, ©RobHainer/Getty Images; 2, ©Matt Benoit/Shutterstock; 3, ©alvarez/Getty Images; 4, ©RichLegg/Getty Images; 5, ©AzmanJaka/iStock; 6, ©Billy Gadbury/Shutterstock; 7, ©Leonard Zhukovsky/Shutterstock; 8, ©GL Archive/Alamy; 9, ©Jim West/Alamy; 10, ©Photo Spirit/Shutterstock; 11, ©Africa Studio/Shutterstock; 12, ©cynoclub/iStock; 13, ©PA Images/Alamy; 14, ©John Roman Images/Shutterstock; 15, ©Portland Press Herald/Getty Images; 16, ©Boston Globe/Getty Images; 17, ©Amit.pansuriya/Shutterstock; 18, ©adogslifephoto/iStock; 19, ©Mikael Karlsson/Alamy; 20, ©Design Pics/Alamy; 21, ©Marmaduke St. John/Alamy; 22, ©Chris Weeks/Getty Images; 23, ©GlobalP/Getty Images

President: Jen Jenson
Director of Product Development: Spencer Brinker
Senior Editor: Allison Juda
Associate Editor: Charly Haley
Designer: Colin O'Dea

Library of Congress Cataloging-in-Publication Data

Names: Peterson, Megan Cooley, author.
Title: Police dogs / by Megan Cooley Peterson.
Description: Minneapolis : Bearport Publishing Company, 2021. | Series: Heroic dogs | Includes bibliographical references and index.
Identifiers: LCCN 2021001088 (print) | LCCN 2021001089 (ebook) | ISBN 9781636911205 (library binding) | ISBN 9781636911298 (paperback) | ISBN 9781636911380 (ebook)
Subjects: LCSH: Police dogs--Juvenile literature.
Classification: LCC HV8025 .P48 2021 (print) | LCC HV8025 (ebook) | DDC 363.2/32--dc23
LC record available at https://lccn.loc.gov/2021001088
LC ebook record available at https://lccn.loc.gov/2021001089

For more information, write to Bearport Publishing, 5357 Penn Avenue South, Minneapolis, MN 55419. Printed in the United States of America.

Police dogs learn what scent to search for by sniffing something that belongs to the missing person.

A Community's Best Friend

The most important job for police dogs is to keep members of the community safe. These dogs are paired with human officers to search for missing people and stolen things. The teams patrol parks, playgrounds, and neighborhoods. Sometimes, police dogs sniff out drugs and other dangerous items. They can even track down **suspects** believed to have broken the law.

Many police dogs have official **badges** that show they are part of the police.

Police dogs work with the same human partners for the whole time they are on the job.

A History of Helping

Dogs have been used to protect communities for hundreds of years. Guard dogs barked to warn their owners about strangers. Sometimes dogs even helped find thieves. The first school for training police dogs opened in Belgium in 1899. Since then, these helpers have risked their lives every day to keep community members and officers safe.

New York City began using police dogs in 1907. It was the first U.S. city to add dogs to its police team.

Police dogs often meet with members of their communities. That way, people can ask questions and learn more about these K-9 officers.

What Makes a Good Police Dog?

Which dogs are cut out for this tough job? The best **candidates** are dogs that are **eager** to learn. They need to listen well and be easy to train. Police dogs also need to be able to **focus**, no matter what is going on around them.

Never pet a police dog without asking for permission first. The dog is working.

Any **breed** of dog can become a police dog, but German shepherds are often picked for the work. Bloodhounds and Labrador retrievers make good police dogs, too.

Passing the Puppy Tests

First up on the journey to finding police dogs, it's time to put promising puppies to the test. Trainers want to see if the animals show signs of the **behaviors** they will need if they become K-9 officers. In one test, trainers watch to see if puppies follow toys after they are taken away. Puppies that stay focused might make good police dogs. Another test sees if puppies can stay calm around loud noises.

Puppy tests are only the first step in police dog training. A dog must learn many other skills before it can work with the police.

These eight-week-old German shepherd puppies are ready for their first test!

Teacher's Pet

For puppies that pass their tests, the next step begins when they are about one year old. They team up with human partners and begin training. The dogs practice climbing walls and jumping through windows. They learn to follow scents and sniff out **evidence**. Training to be a police dog is hard work, but it can be fun, too. The dogs are rewarded with treats and toys when they do well.

Police dogs are trained to perform **alerts** when they find things. They may point with their noses, paw at the ground, or walk circles around human officers.

Dress for Success

Police dogs also need to get used to wearing special gear. They often wear vests or **harnesses** made of tough materials. These keep the dogs safe when they're working in dangerous situations. Police dogs need to train to follow commands, or **cues**, while they are both on and off their leashes.

Police dogs train in the full gear that they will wear when working.

Some police dogs wear goggles made for dogs—doggles! These protect the dogs' eyes from harm while in the line of duty.

The Nose Knows

Vests and doggles are important, but dogs are born with their own special gear—their sniffers! They use their super sense of smell to track down drugs, bombs, or dangerous weapons. Once police dogs find what they were searching for, their human partners take care of the rest.

Bloodhounds have the best sense of smell of all dog breeds. They can follow a scent trail for days.

Smells on the ground don't last long. Police dogs must get to work right away before scents disappear.

Finding People

Sometimes police dogs need to find more than just dangerous objects. Finding people may also be in a day's work. K-9 officers can detect a person's smell by sniffing around. Then, they follow the scent to find the person.

Hot, windy, or rainy weather can make it harder for police dogs to follow smells.

Sometimes, canine officers ride in patrol cars with their human partners.

Police dogs keep up their special skills by training often until they **retire**. Then, they usually live with their human partners who continue to love and care for the pups as pets.

Meet a Real Police Dog

The Los Angeles Police Department works with many police dogs. One of their bravest four-legged officers was a Belgian Malinois named Edo. Edo once helped officers rescue children trapped inside a house! Edo showed no fear in the line of duty. His bravery and skills made him a true police dog hero.

In 2016, Edo was awarded the K-9 Hero of the Year award for saving the trapped children.

Glossary

alerts behaviors used to bring something to a person's attention

badges things worn to show that people or animals belong to a group or do a job

behaviors the ways a person or animal acts or does things

breed a group of dogs that look and act in a similar way

candidates people or animals who are hoping for a certain job

cues words or actions that signal a dog to do something

eager wanting to do something very much

evidence objects or information that can be used to prove whether something is true

focus something one is giving full attention to

harnesses straps with handles worn by dogs that their handlers can hold

retire to stop working, usually because of age

suspects people who are thought to have committed crimes

Index

Read More

Holmes, Parker. *K9 and Military Dogs (Canine Athletes).* Minneapolis: Abdo Publishing, 2019.

Laughlin, Kara L. *Police Dogs (Dogs with Jobs).* New York: AV2 by Weigl, 2019.

Learn More Online

1. Go to **www.factsurfer.com**
2. Enter "**Police Dogs**" into the search box.
3. Click on the cover of this book to see a list of websites.

About the Author

Megan Cooley Peterson is an author and editor. She grew up with two lovable dogs—a German shepherd named Sheba and a golden retriever named Gus. She lives in Minnesota with her husband and daughter.